DEL REY
NEW YORK

ONLINE SAFETY FOR YOUNGER FANS
Spending time online is great fun! Here are a few simple rules to help younger fans stay safe and keep the Internet a great place to spend time:
- Never give out your real name—don't use it as your username.
- Never give out any of your personal details.
- Never tell anybody which school you go to or how old you are.
- Never tell anybody your password except a parent or a guardian.
- Be aware that you must be 13 or over to create an account on many sites. Always check the site policy and ask a parent or guardian for permission before registering.
- Always tell a parent or guardian if something is worrying you.

Copyright © 2019 by Mojang AB and Mojang Synergies AB. MINECRAFT is a trademark or registered trademark of Mojang Synergies AB.

Published in the United States by Del Rey, an imprint of Random House, a division of Penguin Random House LLC, New York.

Published in hardcover in the United Kingdom by Egmont UK Limited.

ISBN 978-0-593-12960-9
Ebook ISBN 978-0-593-12961-6

Printed in China on acid-free paper by C & C Offset

Written by Stephanie Milton

Illustrations by Ryan Marsh

randomhousebooks.com

2 4 6 8 9 7 5 3 1

First US Edition

Design by Design Button Ltd.

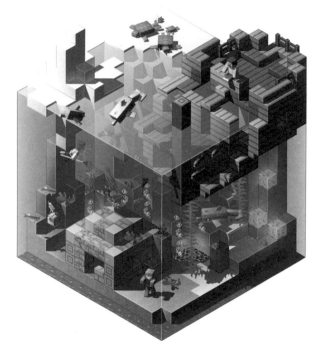

GUITE TO:

 OCEAN SURVIVAL

CONTENTS

1. STRUCTURES AND LOOT

2. OCEAN MOBS

3. SURVIVAL TIPS

INTRODUCTION

Welcome to the official *Guide to Ocean Survival*! Thanks so much for picking up this super guide to all the beautiful and terrible things you'll encounter in the Overworld's seas!

I guess you want to become an aquatic expert, ready to discover the most precious treasures under the waves, identify every weird and wonderful mob and construct amazing underwater builds. Well, you've made a great start!

You probably already know that it can get dangerous down there. You'll need to prepare yourself with special enchantments, potions and items to help you hold your breath and see in the dark. Perhaps you also know about some of the fearsome mobs that lurk in forgotten ruins on the ocean floor? All you need to face them and tell the tale is right here. There are lots of great ideas for show-stopping undersea bases, too. After all, to make the very best of your time in the depths, you need a great place to kick back and relax.

So come on in, it's time to take a deep dive!

ALEX WILTSHIRE
THE MOJANG TEAM

MOJANG STUFF

This super-exclusive info has come directly from the developers at Mojang.

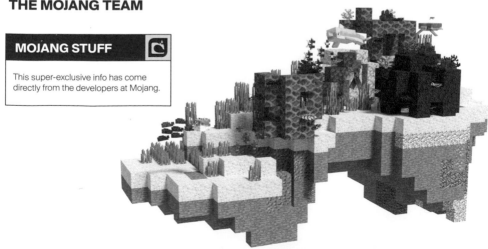

THE OCEAN BIOMES

Once you start to explore, you'll soon realize that not all areas of ocean are the same. In fact, there are several different ocean biomes and each has unique features. Before you dive in, let's take a look at the differences between each ocean biome, so you'll know how to recognize them.

FROZEN OCEAN

You'll know you've strayed into an area of frozen ocean pretty quickly – the water is a dark purple color and the surface is covered in ice. You'll also see icebergs, which are made from blue ice, packed ice and snow. Any underwater ruins you find will be made of stone.

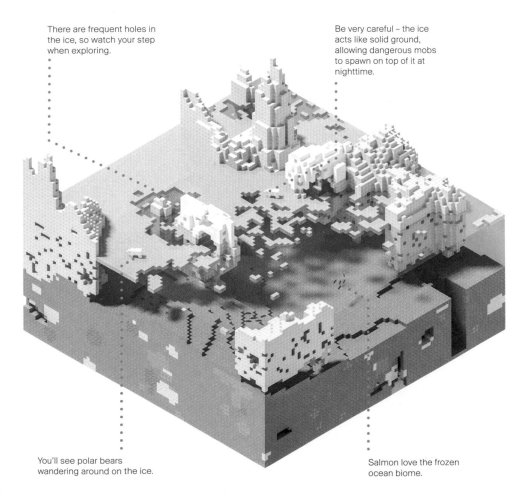

There are frequent holes in the ice, so watch your step when exploring.

Be very careful – the ice acts like solid ground, allowing dangerous mobs to spawn on top of it at nighttime.

You'll see polar bears wandering around on the ice.

Salmon love the frozen ocean biome.

COLD OCEAN

Cold oceans have dark blue water at the surface and the ocean bed is mostly made of gravel. Any underwater ruins will be made of stone blocks, and you'll see some seagrass and kelp.

Salmon like to spawn in these cold waters.

Cod are found here in schools of up to 9.

MOJANG STUFF

We were careful to make sure the ruins you find in cold and warm ocean biomes look different, to make them interesting to discover as you explore.

You'll see patches of dirt, clay and sand among the gravel.

LUKEWARM OCEAN

Light-blue surface water is the first sign that you're in a lukewarm area of ocean. The ocean bed is made of sand, and kelp and seagrass thrive here. Any underwater ruins you find will be made of sandy blocks rather than stone.

The seabed is composed of dirt, clay and gravel among the sand.

Tropical fish like to spawn in these warmer waters.

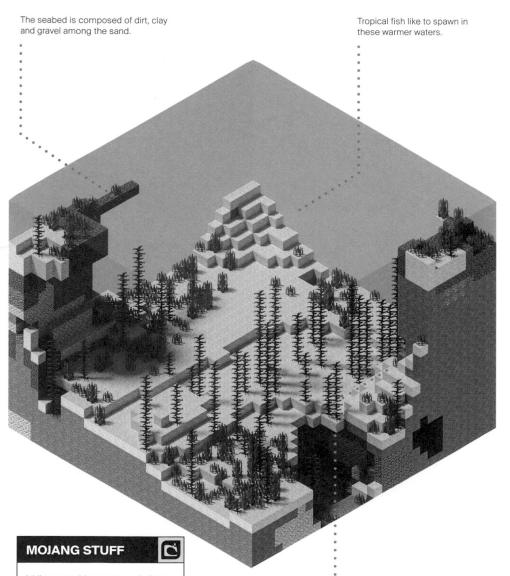

Pufferfish may spawn in lukewarm oceans, in groups of 3-5.

WARM OCEAN

The water at the surface of warm areas of ocean is an inviting, light green color, and the ocean floor is sandy. There's plenty of seagrass, but no kelp. Like lukewarm areas, the underwater ruins here will be made of sandy blocks.

Tropical fish love warm ocean biomes, so you'll see plenty of them here.

Warm oceans are the only biome in which you'll find coral reefs.

Pufferfish also love warm ocean biomes, although they're rarer than tropical fish.

DID YOU KNOW?

There is a deep version of each ocean biome and vast ocean monuments may generate in these deep waters. Monuments contain hidden treasure, as well as dangerous hostile mobs known as guardians and elder guardians. Learn more about ocean monuments on pages 34-35.

BEFORE YOU DIVE IN

Now that you know how to recognize the different types of ocean, you're almost ready to begin your first aquatic adventure! But before you dive in, you need to make sure you're ready for what awaits. There are several special items that are essential to your survival, including potions and enchanted equipment.

FOOD

You'll need to take some good quality food with you on your underwater escapade so you can replenish your health and hunger bars. In general, meat is better than fruits and vegetables, as it restores more hunger points, and cooked meat is more nourishing than raw meat. Steak is always a good option as each piece restores 8 hunger points. Cooked pork chops will restore 8 hunger points apiece, too. Cake is another good idea – each cake has 7 slices and each slice restores 2 hunger points.

WOOD

Wood is an essential crafting ingredient and you'll want to have a few stacks in your inventory at all times so you can craft replacement tools and weapons when necessary. In an emergency, you can mine wood from any shipwrecks you come across – they're constructed almost entirely from wood and wood planks.

POTION OF WATER BREATHING

When drunk, each bottle of this handy potion allows you to breathe underwater for 3 minutes rather than the usual 15 seconds. Just brew a pufferfish with awkward potion. For the extended version, which lasts 8 minutes, brew potion of water breathing with redstone.

AWKWARD POTION RECIPE

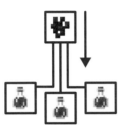

WATER BREATHING RECIPE

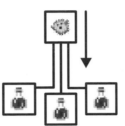

WATER BREATHING (EXTENDED) RECIPE

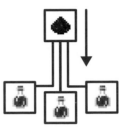

POTION OF NIGHT VISION

It's murky down in the ocean depths, so you'll need potion of night vision to bring everything back to maximum light level. Brew awkward potion with a golden carrot to make night vision – each bottle lasts 3 minutes. You can extend this to 8 minutes by brewing potion of night vision with redstone.

POTION OF REGENERATION

This potion will restore your health by around 2 health points every 2.4 seconds. Each potion lasts for 45 seconds. Brew awkward potion with a ghast tear to make it. For the extended version, which lasts for 1 minute 30 seconds, brew potion of regeneration with redstone.

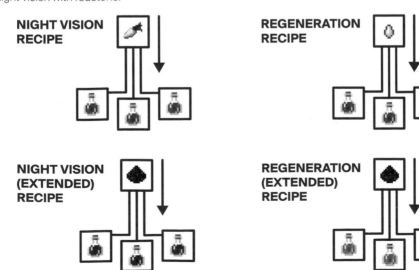

NIGHT VISION RECIPE

REGENERATION RECIPE

NIGHT VISION (EXTENDED) RECIPE

REGENERATION (EXTENDED) RECIPE

RESPIRATION HELMET

Enchant your helmet with respiration on an enchantment table and each level will increase your underwater breathing time by 15 seconds.

DEPTH STRIDER BOOTS

This is a good enchantment for your boots because your movement is slower when you're underwater. Each level of the enchantment reduces the amount that water slows you down by a third – so by level 3 (the maximum level) you'll be able to swim as quickly as you can walk on land.

TURTLE SHELL

Have you spotted any turtles during your land-based adventures? When they're not swimming in the ocean, these passive mobs can often be seen in groups on warm, sandy beaches. When they become adults, baby turtles drop an item called a scute. Collect 5 scutes and you'll be able to craft a turtle shell – a helmet that provides the wearer with the water breathing effect.

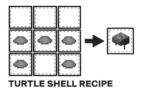

TURTLE SHELL RECIPE

FROST WALKER BOOTS

It's worth keeping a pair of frost walker boots in your inventory if you're serious about exploring large areas of ocean. That way, if you want to travel across a large expanse of ocean quickly, you can simply run across the surface and your boots will create frosted blocks of ice under your feet as you travel. Just bear in mind that if you stop moving, the ice will gradually melt.

LOOTING SWORD

Enchant your sword with looting, and hostile underwater mobs will drop more items when defeated. They'll also be more likely to drop uncommon and rare items, as well as any equipment they may be holding or wearing. An iron sword is good, but a diamond sword is better if you have enough materials.

EFFICIENCY PICKAXE

The efficiency enchantment will allow you to mine blocks more quickly than usual. It's very useful when you're mining underwater and can be applied to your shovel and axe as well as your pickaxe. Make sure you're using the correct tool for the block you're mining, otherwise the effect won't work – use a pickaxe for stone or a shovel for gravel.

1

STRUCTURES AND LOOT

There are all sorts of mysterious structures waiting to be explored in the ocean. Although they may be crawling with dangerous mobs, they also contain valuable items and rare treasures. In this section we'll explore these structures and find out where to search for loot.

FISHING

There are many rare treasures to be found in the ocean, and some of them can be retrieved from the relative safety of a boat. Let's take a look at how fishing works and discover what you might reel in on a very good day.

1 Craft a fishing rod. You'll just need sticks and string.

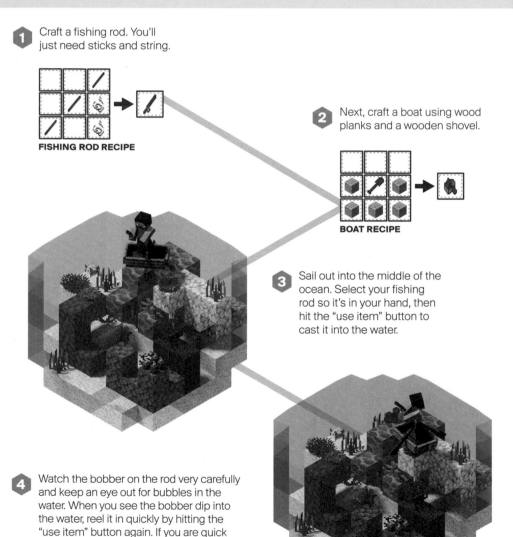

FISHING ROD RECIPE

2 Next, craft a boat using wood planks and a wooden shovel.

BOAT RECIPE

3 Sail out into the middle of the ocean. Select your fishing rod so it's in your hand, then hit the "use item" button to cast it into the water.

4 Watch the bobber on the rod very carefully and keep an eye out for bubbles in the water. When you see the bobber dip into the water, reel it in quickly by hitting the "use item" button again. If you are quick enough, the item you just caught will appear in your hotbar or inventory.

WHAT YOU CAN CATCH

There's more than just fish in these waters! You might also reel in junk or treasure items while fishing. Here's a complete list of all the possible items you might find on the end of your rod.

Raw cod	Raw salmon	Tropical fish	Pufferfish	Bow
Enchanted book	Fishing rod	Name tag	Nautilus shell	Saddle
Lily pad	Bamboo	Bowl	Leather	Leather boots
Rotten flesh	Stick	String	Water bottle	Bone
Ink sac	Tripwire hook			

TIP

To increase the chance of reeling in treasure items and reduce the chance of reeling in junk items, enchant your fishing rod with luck of the sea using your enchantment table.

THE OCEAN FLOOR

The ocean floor is home to a variety of blocks and plant life. In many ways it's similar to the land above sea level – different blocks and plants appear in different areas and it's worth taking some time to explore.

1 SAND AND GRAVEL
These two blocks cover large areas of ocean floor. Gravel covers the floor in cold areas of ocean and sand covers the floor in warm areas of ocean.

2 CAVES
The ocean floor is very similar to the terrain above sea level – it's hilly and you'll find lots of caves to explore. Be careful – some lead to caves that aren't flooded by water, so you'll bump into lots of dangerous mobs like zombies and creepers.

3 SEAGRASS
Seagrass grows in all types of ocean except for frozen ocean. If you want it to drop as an item, you'll need to mine it with shears. You can use seagrass to breed turtles.

4 KELP
Kelp grows in all areas of ocean except for warm ocean. It can be mined with any tool or by hand. Smelt kelp in a furnace to make dried kelp – this food item restores 1 hunger point. Craft 9 dried kelp into a block of dried kelp, which can be used for decoration.

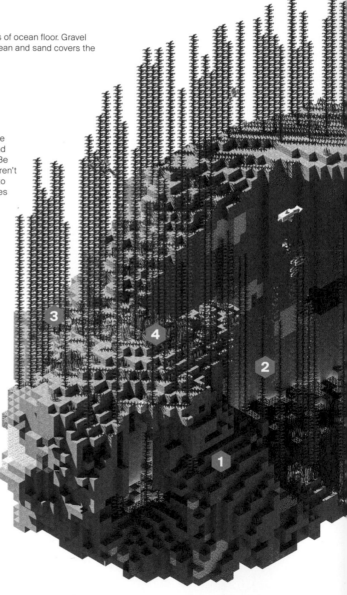

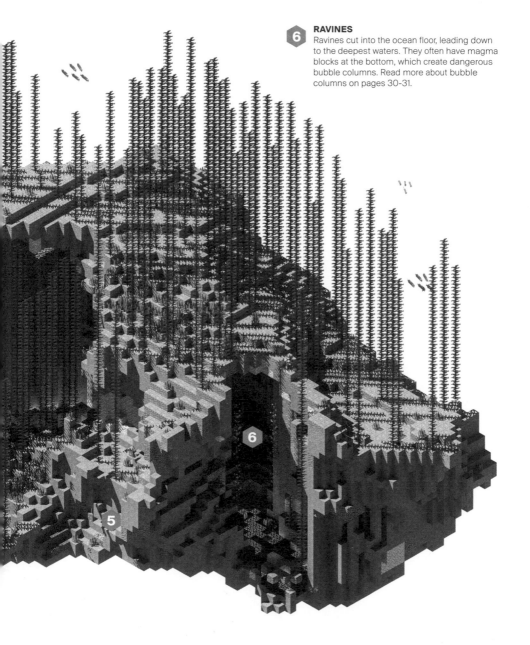

STONE AND ORES

All varieties of stone can be found on the ocean floor and inside caves and ravines. Valuable ore blocks like coal, iron and gold can be seen running through the stone in rich veins.

RAVINES

Ravines cut into the ocean floor, leading down to the deepest waters. They often have magma blocks at the bottom, which create dangerous bubble columns. Read more about bubble columns on pages 30-31.

SHIPWRECKS

You're likely to see several shipwrecks on your underwater adventures – they appear in all areas of the ocean. They're worth checking out whenever you see one – you can find some valuable items inside, and you can turn them into underwater bases, too, so you have somewhere to take shelter.

UPRIGHT

Shipwrecks look a bit like pirate ships.

They're often missing their bow, stern and mast, but occasionally you'll find a ship in one piece.

Supply chests contain everything from potatoes to TNT.

DID YOU KNOW?

Shipwrecks may also generate above sea level, on beaches. Sometimes you'll even spot one in a river!

SIDEWAYS

Shipwrecks are mainly built out of wood blocks. You'll find wood, wood planks, fences, stairs, trapdoors and doors.

Treasure chests contain everything from iron ingots to diamonds.

Map chests contain buried treasure maps, which will lead you to buried treasure chests. Find out more about those on pages 26-27!

UPSIDE-DOWN

You'll find 1-3 chests hidden inside each shipwreck - these could be supply chests, map chests or treasure chests.

UNDERWATER RUINS

Mysterious underwater ruins are a common sight on the ocean floor. Nobody knows the story behind these structures – perhaps they were once villages that fell victim to rising sea levels....There are several types of ruin to explore – let's discover what you'll find in each.

COLD UNDERWATER RUINS

1 Cold underwater ruins are found in frozen and cold areas of ocean.

2 Most cold ruins contain loot chests. Inside you might find anything from emeralds to a buried treasure map.

3 They vary in size – you'll discover everything from small huts to large towers.

4 Ruins often generate together in what look like small villages.

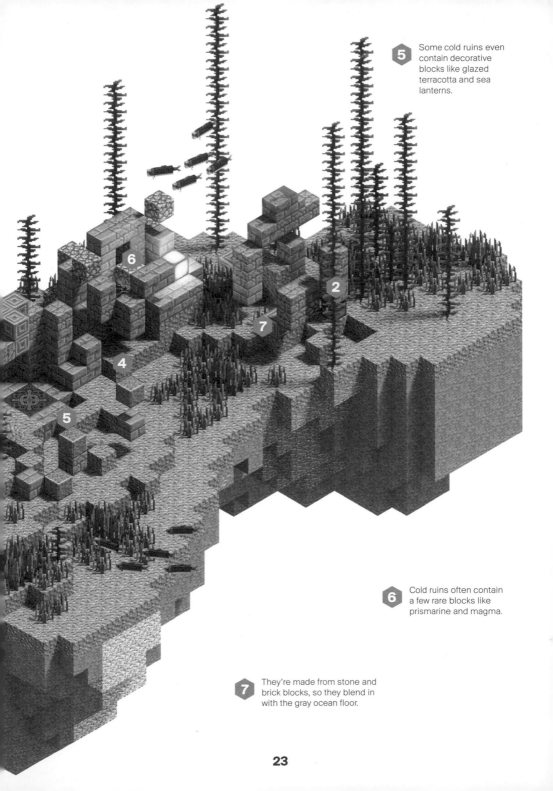

5 Some cold ruins even contain decorative blocks like glazed terracotta and sea lanterns.

6 Cold ruins often contain a few rare blocks like prismarine and magma.

7 They're made from stone and brick blocks, so they blend in with the gray ocean floor.

WARM UNDERWATER RUINS

1 Warm underwater ruins can be found in lukewarm and warm areas of ocean.

3

1

2 Like cold ruins, most warm ruins contain loot chests, and you might find a buried treasure map inside.

3 Warm ruins often have blocks like polished granite and polished diorite.

4 They're made from sand and sandstone blocks, so they blend in with the sandy ocean floor.

TIP

You can turn ruins into emergency underwater bases so you have somewhere safe to retreat to if things get difficult.

4

2

5

5 You'll often see damaged arches in between the ruins.

DID YOU KNOW?

Occasionally, underwater ruins will appear on land, where the ocean meets the shore.

BURIED TREASURE

Once you've found a buried treasure map in a shipwreck or a ruin, you can set off on a quest to locate a buried treasure chest. Follow these steps and you'll soon find yourself the proud owner of some very valuable treasure.

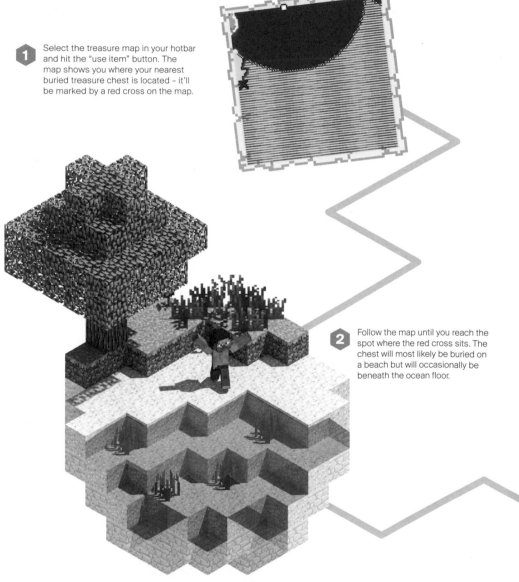

1 Select the treasure map in your hotbar and hit the "use item" button. The map shows you where your nearest buried treasure chest is located – it'll be marked by a red cross on the map.

2 Follow the map until you reach the spot where the red cross sits. The chest will most likely be buried on a beach but will occasionally be beneath the ocean floor.

5 Buried treasure chests will
also contain several other
items of loot like emeralds,
diamonds and prismarine
crystals. Be sure to grab
these, too!

4 These chests are the only place you'll find the heart of the sea, a
very rare item. Each chest contains one of these, and you'll need
it to craft a conduit – a valuable block that will help you survive
underwater. Learn more about conduits on pages 56-59.

3 Dig around the spot marked
on the map until you find the
chest. It's usually hidden by
blocks of sand or gravel.

ICEBERGS

As you would expect, icebergs are only found in areas of frozen ocean. They're made from several different blocks of ice, and snow has usually settled on top of them, too. Here are some interesting facts about icebergs.

 Icebergs are made from a combination of packed ice, ice and blue ice.

 Icebergs sometimes have small holes in them that look like caves. These holes will occasionally cut through the entire iceberg and come out the other side.

3 The majority of the iceberg is submerged in the ocean. Dive under the ice to see for yourself!

 They come in a variety of shapes and sizes – some look like small islands, others look like mountains.

4

5 You can hollow out an iceberg and turn it into a base if you need to hide from dangerous mobs.

5

6

6 Dangerous mobs walk around on icebergs and the ice surrounding them.

BUBBLE COLUMNS

If you see a stream of bubbles emerging from a ravine, be very careful! They may look innocent, but they can be deadly, as they can push and pull players in different directions. Here's everything you need to know about bubble columns.

1 Lava forms in deep areas of the ocean. When lava forms underwater, some of it turns to magma and some turns to obsidian.

3

1

2

 Ravines often have magma and obsidian blocks at the very bottom.

 Magma blocks create bubbles when they're in water. These bubbles travel downward and they're known as whirlpool bubble columns.

4 Whirlpool bubble columns can drag players down to the bottom of the ravine, where they can take damage from the magma and drown.

4

5

6

5 If you travel over a whirlpool bubble column in a boat, your boat will begin to shake and then sink.

6 If you're careful, you can also enter bubble columns to replenish your air supply.

CORAL REEFS

As you're exploring warm oceans, you're likely to come across a colorful coral reef. This vast structure is teeming with life and is the only place you'll find coral. Let's explore a coral reef in more detail.

1 CORAL BLOCKS

You'll see clusters of colorful coral blocks all over the reef. There are five types: tube (blue), brain (pink), bubble (purple), fire (red) and horn (yellow). Coral blocks make great decoration for your builds, but one of the blocks surrounding each block of coral must be water or they will turn into dead coral.

3 MINING CORAL

You must mine coral blocks and coral fans with a pickaxe enchanted with silk touch if you want to collect them – if you mine them with a regular pickaxe they'll drop dead coral instead. Coral blocks can be used as decoration in your builds, but one of the blocks surrounding each block of coral must be water or they will turn into dead coral.

2 CORAL FANS

On top of coral blocks, you'll see another type of coral – coral fans. These come in the same five variants as coral blocks. Like the block version, coral can be used as a decoration in your builds, but if it isn't placed in water it will turn to dead coral within a matter of seconds.

TIP

If you find yourself being attacked by drowned mobs, you can hollow out one of the larger coral outcrops and make a colorful emergency base.

4 DEAD CORAL

You'll also see some gray coral blocks and coral fans among all the color – this is dead coral.

5 SEA PICKLES

Sea pickles are tiny, light-emitting animals. They like to live on top of coral and on the seabed in warm oceans. They can be mined by hand or with any tool. You can place sea pickles on top of solid blocks, but they'll only emit light when underwater.

OCEAN MONUMENTS

Ocean monuments are the largest structures in the ocean, which is why you'll only find them in the deepest waters. They're very dangerous, but worth exploring as they contain some valuable loot.

 Ocean monuments are built in the shape of a pyramid, from prismarine, prismarine bricks and dark prismarine blocks.

 They're lit up with sea lanterns – these blocks are the only source of light in monuments.

 The monument is supported by giant pillars that sit on the ocean floor.

 Inside, you'll find lots of narrow corridors leading to various chambers. Be careful in the corridors – you can easily find yourself surrounded by dangerous mobs.

The most important chamber for explorers is the treasure chamber. Inside, encased in dark prismarine, you'll find 8 solid gold blocks.

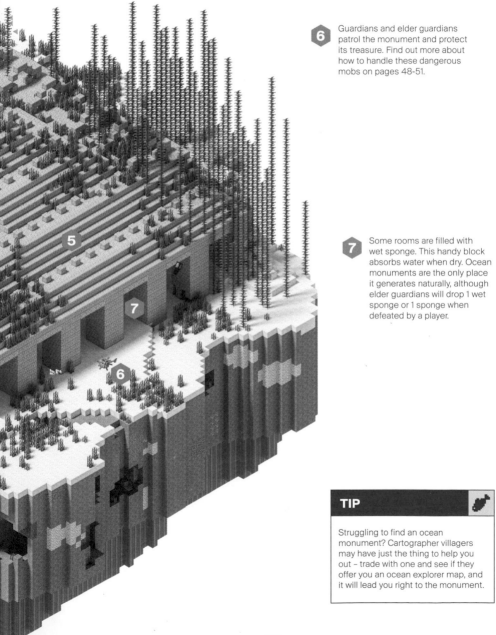

Guardians and elder guardians patrol the monument and protect its treasure. Find out more about how to handle these dangerous mobs on pages 48-51.

Some rooms are filled with wet sponge. This handy block absorbs water when dry. Ocean monuments are the only place it generates naturally, although elder guardians will drop 1 wet sponge or 1 sponge when defeated by a player.

TIP

Struggling to find an ocean monument? Cartographer villagers may have just the thing to help you out – trade with one and see if they offer you an ocean explorer map, and it will lead you right to the monument.

OCEAN MOBS

As we've seen, Minecraft's oceans are full of life – some of it is friendly and some of it is extremely dangerous. In this section we'll take a closer look at the creatures you'll meet beneath the water so you can recognize friend from foe.

FISH

Wherever you go in the ocean, you're sure to see plenty of fish. These passive mobs come in several different varieties and they each behave in different ways. Let's find out where you'll find each one and what they drop.

 COD
You'll find cod in normal, lukewarm and cold areas of ocean. They like to swim in groups of up to 9. They drop 1 raw cod when defeated, which restores 2 food points, and 5 food points if cooked.

 SALMON
Salmon spawn in cold and frozen oceans, and will also spawn in rivers. There are 3 sizes: small, regular and large. They swim around in groups of 3-5. Salmon are also capable of swimming up waterfalls. They drop 1 raw salmon when defeated, which restores 2 food points, and 6 food points if cooked.

 PUFFERFISH
Pufferfish prefer lukewarm and warm oceans and can often be found hiding in coral reefs. Pufferfish can be defensive and will puff up when near hostile mobs. If you approach a pufferfish when it's puffed up, it will inflict 7 seconds of poison, and if you touch it, you'll take more damage. Like salmon, they can also swim up waterfalls. They drop 1 pufferfish when defeated – it's not a good idea to eat pufferfish as they inflict hunger, poison and nausea. They do, however, come in handy for brewing a potion of water breathing.

TROPICAL FISH

Tropical fish only spawn in lukewarm and warm oceans. There are 22 common varieties, but there are 2 possible shapes, 15 colors, 6 patterns and 15 pattern color options, giving a total of 2,700 possible combinations! They will drop 1 tropical fish when defeated, which restores 1 food point.

FISH BUCKETS

This handy item allows you to transport fish from one place to another, which means you can make your very own aquarium! If you use a water bucket or an empty bucket on a fish, the fish will be scooped up into the bucket, turning it into a fish bucket. To place the fish back into the world, just hit the "use item" button.

SQUID

HEALTH POINTS	❤	10
ATTACK STRENGTH	❤	0
ITEMS DROPPED		
	1-3	1-3

SPAWN LOCATION
In any area of ocean.

OCEAN

MOJANG STUFF

During Beta, squids didn't despawn when you moved away from them, so players kept them as pets! We had to change that, though, because at the time they could only swim downward and they'd collect in writhing masses on the seabed that wouldn't go away...

BEHAVIOR

These passive creatures spawn in the ocean in groups of up to 4. They propel themselves through the water using their tentacles. They have a large mouth full of teeth on their underside – this can sometimes alarm explorers, but squid are harmless and will never use their teeth to hurt you. They can't survive out of water and will suffocate if beached.

USEFUL DROPS

As well as experience points, squid drop 1-3 ink sacs when defeated, which can be used to dye things black. Try crafting a bed or glass with an ink sac to see the result.

SPECIAL SKILLS

Squid can produce a cloud of black ink as a defense mechanism when attacked. This obscures their attacker's vision, allowing them to escape. They will swim away from a player or a guardian if attacked.

TURTLES

HEALTH POINTS	30
ATTACK STRENGTH	0
ITEMS DROPPED	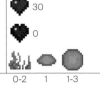

0-2   1   1-3

SPAWN LOCATION
On warm beaches.

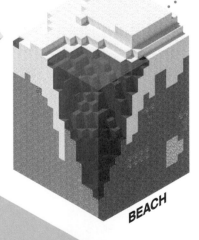

BEACH

MOJANG STUFF

The idea for the turtle originally came from Reddit user billyK_, who mounted a two-year campaign for them as a replacement for boats and suggested their shells could be used as helmets.

TIP

Undead mobs like zombies, drowned and skeletons will try to stamp on turtle eggs and will attack baby turtles, too. Wild ocelots and wild wolves will also attack baby turtles. Keep an eye out for these mobs and make sure you fend them off before they do any damage.

BEHAVIOR

Turtles spawn in small groups. They are strong swimmers and can often be seen exploring the ocean, but move much more slowly on land. They are passive and will retreat if attacked by a player or other mob.

USEFUL DROPS

Turtles may drop up to 2 pieces of seagrass when defeated, but nobody wants to see such a sad event. Baby turtles drop a scute when they grow up, and this can be used to craft a turtle shell. See page 12 for a reminder of the recipe.

SPECIAL SKILLS

Feed 2 turtles seagrass and they will breed. One of the turtles will then return to its home beach (the beach where it spawned), find a sand block and lay 1-4 turtle eggs. These take a while to hatch so you'll need to keep an eye on them over a period of a few days and nights. They go through two stages of cracking before finally hatching to reveal a baby turtle.

DOLPHINS

HEALTH POINTS	10	
ATTACK STRENGTH	2-4	
ITEMS DROPPED	0-1	

SPAWN LOCATION

Dolphins spawn in all areas of ocean except for frozen ocean.

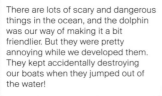

OCEAN

MOJANG STUFF

There are lots of scary and dangerous things in the ocean, and the dolphin was our way of making it a bit friendlier. But they were pretty annoying while we developed them. They kept accidentally destroying our boats when they jumped out of the water!

BEHAVIOR

Dolphins are intelligent and friendly. They swim around in large groups and can often be seen jumping in and out of the water. They will avoid guardians and elder guardians. They need air every so often but can't survive for long out of the water. If they find themselves on land, they will try to find a body of water.

USEFUL DROPS

In the unfortunate event of a dolphin's demise, they may drop 1 raw cod. It's something to be avoided, so make sure you do everything you can to keep the dolphins happy!

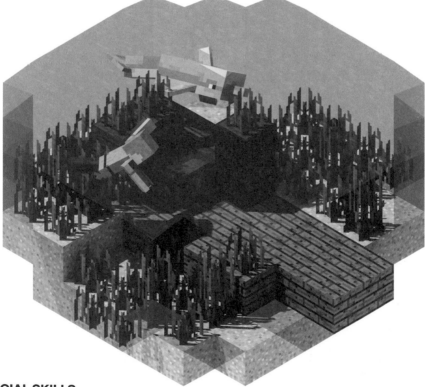

SPECIAL SKILLS

Dolphins have been known to chase after players in boats. They can also give a speed boost to players who swim near them. If you drop an item in the ocean, dolphins will come over to investigate – they'll knock the item around and chase after it. If you attack a dolphin, the entire group will become hostile toward the attacker. If you feed dolphins raw cod or raw salmon, they will begin to trust you, which means they'll interact with you more. Once you've fed them, they'll lead you to the nearest loot chest in an underwater ruin or shipwreck to say thank you.

DROWNED

HEALTH POINTS	20		
ATTACK STRENGTH	2-9		
HOW TO DEFEAT			
ITEMS DROPPED	0-2	0-1	0-1	5

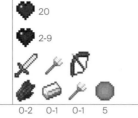

MOJANG STUFF

We made sure that the drowned really don't like being far from water. If, during the day, they're prevented from being able to get back to water, they become passive. Once they get soggy again they'll return to fighting form.

SPAWN LOCATION

In all areas of ocean except for warm ocean, as well as rivers and swamps.

OCEAN

BEHAVIOR

Drowned mobs spawn in water at light levels of 7 or lower. They also spawn in rivers and swamps. Like zombies, they will attack you with their hands. They will come up onto dry land at night, where they will stomp on turtle eggs and attack baby turtles as well as players. They will also chase after villagers and iron golems.

SPECIAL SKILLS

Drowned may spawn with a tridcnt – a powerful weapon that can be thrown at enemies. They may also spawn with a fishing rod, or with a nautilus shell, which is needed to craft a conduit. More about conduits on pages 56-59.

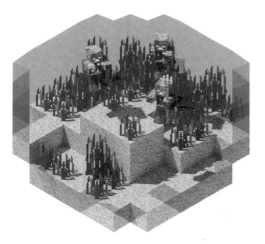

USEFUL DROPS

Drowned may drop their trident if they're holding one. Find more about this weapon on pages 54-55. They may also drop a gold ingot.

HOW TO DEFEAT

Hit the drowned with a diamond sword. You can also use its own weapon against it and attack it with a trident, or use a bow.

DID YOU KNOW?

Drowned are a variant of zombies. If a zombie is submerged in water for 30 seconds it will turn into a drowned. You'll know this is happening if the submerged zombie starts to shake.

GUARDIANS

HEALTH POINTS	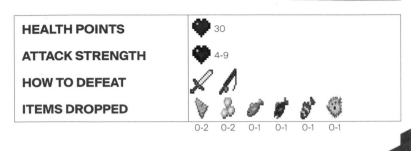 30	
ATTACK STRENGTH	4-9	
HOW TO DEFEAT		
ITEMS DROPPED		

0-2 0-2 0-1 0-1 0-1 0-1

SPAWN LOCATION

In and around ocean monuments in areas of deep ocean.

OCEAN MONUMENT

MOJANG STUFF

Jeb was inspired by his favorite monsters from other games, such as the beholder from Dungeons and Dragons and the fearsome cacodemon from Doom. He just loves those giant floating eye-beasts!

BEHAVIOR

Guardians are found swimming around ocean monuments – their job is to protect the treasure inside the monuments. They attack players and squid on sight, shooting a laser that deals 4-9 points of damage, depending on the level of difficulty your game is set to. This laser has a range of up to 15 blocks. Guardians can also attack with their spikes, which can deal 2 points of damage.

USEFUL DROPS

Guardians may drop prismarine shards or prismarine crystals, which can be crafted into blocks of prismarine and sea lanterns. They may also drop raw fish, although this is rare.

HOW TO DEFEAT

Hit the guardian repeatedly with a diamond sword or stand on land and use a fishing rod to pull it out of the water, then hit it with your diamond sword.

SPECIAL SKILLS

Guardians can live out of water, although they won't be happy about it – they'll squeak angrily at any nearby players and flop around, trying to find water.

ELDER GUARDIANS

HOSTILITY

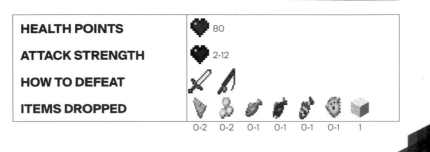

HEALTH POINTS	80	
ATTACK STRENGTH	2-12	
HOW TO DEFEAT		
ITEMS DROPPED		

0-2	0-2	0-1	0-1	0-1	0-1	1

SPAWN LOCATION
Inside ocean monuments.

OCEAN MONUMENT

MOJANG STUFF

The elder guardian's mining fatigue effect was Jeb's solution to prevent players from simply mining their way through the ocean monument to get to its precious loot!

BEHAVIOR

You'll find three elder guardians inside each ocean monument – one in the top room and one in each of the two wings. They are also there to guard the monument's treasure. They attack players on sight with the same laser attack as guardians.

SPECIAL SKILLS

Elder guardians can inflict mining fatigue III on players who dare to venture into the monument. You'll know this is happening to you if a ghostly version of the elder guardian begins to circle you. The effect lasts for 5 minutes – any blocks you mine will break more slowly and your attack speed is reduced. Like guardians, elder guardians won't suffocate on dry land.

USEFUL DROPS

Elder guardians will drop 1 sponge block when defeated. Sponge blocks absorb water so they can be used to clear water from your underwater base.

HOW TO DEFEAT

Hit the elder guardian with your diamond sword or stand on land and use a fishing rod to pull it out of the water, then hit it with your diamond sword.

SURVIVAL TIPS

Now that we've explored the ocean's structures and mobs, it's clear that the ocean is a very dangerous place. But fear not! This section is full of survival tips, from how to enchant a trident and craft a conduit to building an underwater farm.

TRIDENTS

Tridents can't be crafted – you'll only be able to get your hands on one if a drowned mob drops it when defeated. This rare and powerful weapon can be used in hand-to-hand combat or from a distance to take out your foes. Let's find out how it works – it's going to make your life much easier.

MELEE ATTACK

Melee means hand-to-hand or close-quarters combat. If you hit the "use item" button while holding a trident, you will deal 2 points more damage than if you were holding a diamond sword.

RANGED ATTACK

Hold down the "use item" button for a few seconds to charge your trident and aim it at the mob or player you want to attack. When you release the button, the trident will be launched toward your target. If it makes contact with a mob or player, it will bounce off them and fall to the ground nearby. If it hits a block, it will become embedded in that block.

ENCHANTING YOUR TRIDENT

You can enchant a trident on an enchantment table to give it several useful effects. Let's take a look at each effect and how it can help you.

CHANNELING
This only works during thunderstorms. It summons a lightning bolt when a mob is hit by a thrown trident, so the mob is set on fire.

RIPTIDE
It will drag you in the direction the trident is thrown. If you hit a mob or another player, they will be dealt damage. You can use this enchantment to travel to out-of-reach spots.

MENDING
This allows you to repair your trident using your experience points. Hold the trident in your hand, and any experience points you collect will repair the item – 2 durability points are repaired per experience point.

LOYALTY
The loyalty enchantment makes your trident come back to you after you've thrown it. This is very handy – you don't want to lose such a valuable weapon!

IMPALING
Impaling will add 2.5 extra damage points to each hit for aquatic mobs – that's dolphins, fish, squid, turtles, elder guardians and guardians. It won't work on drowned mobs as they're classed as undead.

UNBREAKING
This effect increases your trident's durability so it will last longer – like other tools and weapons, a trident will eventually break.

CONDUITS

Wouldn't it be brilliant if there was a way to breathe, see and mine quickly while underwater, without having to rely on enchantments and potions? That's where the conduit comes in – this clever block acts like a beacon and provides you with these abilities when you're within range.

1 To craft a conduit you'll need 8 nautilus shells and 1 heart of the sea. Nautilus shells are sometimes dropped by drowned mobs and can be caught when fishing. You can find a heart of the sea in every buried treasure chest.

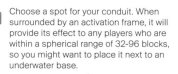

2 Choose a spot for your conduit. When surrounded by an activation frame, it will provide its effect to any players who are within a spherical range of 32-96 blocks, so you might want to place it next to an underwater base.

3 Place your conduit in the center of a 3 x 3 cube of water. Try building a few blocks up from the ocean floor in your chosen spot, placing the conduit on top of these blocks, then removing them so the conduit is floating in position.

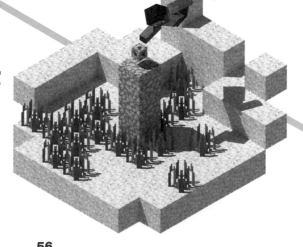

DID YOU KNOW?

Conduits also give off light. They provide a light level of 15, which is the maximum possible and the equivalent of full daylight.

As an added bonus, if you build
all 3 rings, the conduit will attack
any hostile mobs that come within
8 blocks of it, dealing 4 points of
damage every 2 seconds.

5 You'll know you built your activation frame
correctly when the conduit block expands
to reveal its heart of the sea core and
begins to move. You'll also hear what
sounds like a heartbeat. You'll be able to
breathe underwater, see clearly and mine
quickly while you're within range.

 Surround this 3 x 3 cube of water with
up to 3 square rings, each 5 x 5 blocks,
centered around the conduit. The rings
must be made from prismarine, dark
prismarine, prismarine bricks or sea
lanterns, so you'll need to visit an ocean
monument before you can build the
frame. One square ring is enough to
activate the conduit, but 3 will maximize
the conduit's power.

CONDUIT STRUCTURES

Conduits will soon become essential to your underwater adventures. So why not build something a little more permanent for them to sit in? Here are some fun conduit structure ideas for you to try.

THE TREASURE CHEST

The heart of the sea is one of the ocean's most valuable treasures, so why not place your conduit inside a treasure chest? This one's built from wood planks as a nod to the many shipwrecks on the ocean floor. The insides are lined with prismarine and some solid blocks of gold, diamond and emerald.

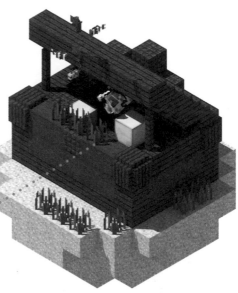

Cover parts of the chest in seagrass to make it feel overgrown.

THE TREE

Trees don't grow under the ocean, so this structure will really add some drama. It's built from various prismarine blocks and looks like a new, aquatic variety of tree. The blocks are placed strategically so that they activate the conduit without forming solid rings.

Dark prismarine has been used to build the trunk, while regular prismarine looks great for the leaves.

THE TOWER

For this design, simply build your conduit activation structure on top of a decorative pillar. This pillar is made from a combination of prismarine blocks and quartz, with some mossy stone bricks for variety.

Sea lanterns are a fitting light source for this tower.

Slab blocks and wall blocks help add smaller details.

THE THRONE

Set your conduit in pride of place on top of this giant prismarine throne. Prismarine stair blocks are useful for creating smaller details for the back and sides of the throne, as well as steps at the front leading up to the conduit.

DID YOU KNOW?

It's possible to activate a conduit without using the exact activation frame design on pages 56-57. As long as there are 16 blocks around the 3 x 3 cube of water, the conduit will still be activated.

CORAL HOUSE

Now that you're an experienced underwater explorer, why not make yourself a more permanent base of operations on the ocean floor? This colorful coral house build is the perfect underwater starter home, and it's dry inside! Follow these steps to build your own coral house.

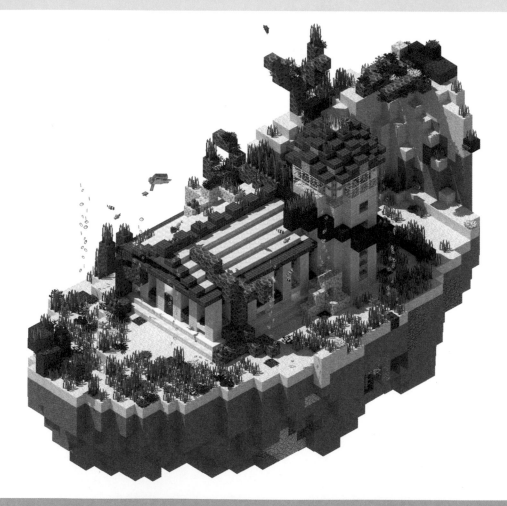

YOU WILL NEED:

SCHEMATICS

These plans show the coral house from various perspectives so you can see how it's constructed. It's built from various sand, prismarine and coral blocks. Inside there are two floors, with plenty of space for all your underwater supplies.

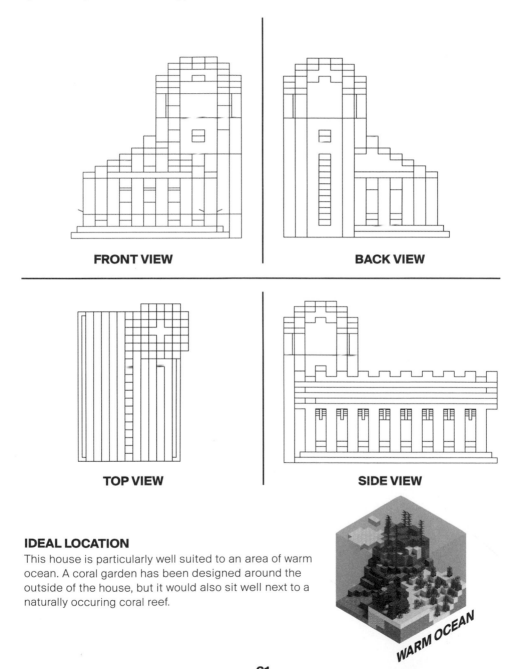

FRONT VIEW

BACK VIEW

TOP VIEW

SIDE VIEW

IDEAL LOCATION

This house is particularly well suited to an area of warm ocean. A coral garden has been designed around the outside of the house, but it would also sit well next to a naturally occuring coral reef.

WARM OCEAN

CORAL HOUSE EXTERIOR

1 The combination of blocks used to build this house helps it blend into the seabed and coral reefs.

2 You enter the house through two separate oak doors connected to a short entrance hall. Don't worry – the doors act as a barrier and will stop water rushing into the house when you open them.

3 Coral, seagrass and kelp are planted around the exterior of the house to create a garden. Blocks of soul sand are hidden around the garden to create upward-moving bubble columns.

4 The windows provide a clear view of the surrounding area. They're made from glass blocks and positioned at various heights across the build.

5 Coral fans placed on slab blocks make colorful window boxes. We've used a combination of prismarine slabs and quartz slabs.

6 Sea lanterns are the perfect light source for this house. They've been placed underneath the overhanging eaves of the roof to light up the exterior of the house.

CORAL HOUSE INTERIOR

 This house has a large ground floor, which is divided into different areas. There's also a tower that is accessible via a ladder.

 Sea lanterns are the perfect lighting for the interior, too. Some are built into the ceiling, others into the walls and floor.

 Use sponge blocks to absorb the water inside the house so you don't have to worry about breathing. Keep placing them until all the water has been absorbed.

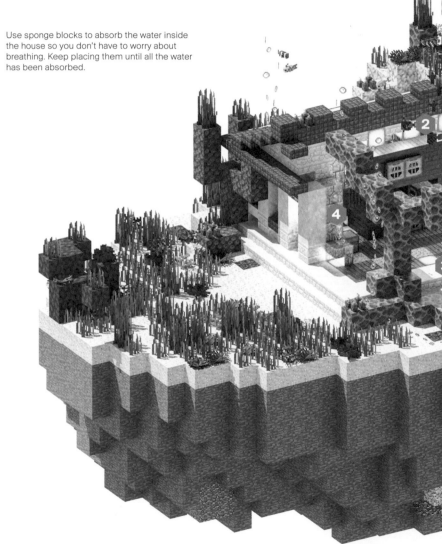

Set up a crafting area in an easily accessible part of your house. You'll need a crafting table, a furnace and a chest for supplies, so you can put everything you collect on your underwater adventures to good use.

 The floor is lined with sponge blocks. This works well with the ocean theme and acts as a flood prevention feature: if water is accidentally let into your house, some of it will be absorbed by the sponge.

6 Make sure you have everything you need to enchant your trident or quickly brew potions of water breathing and night vision. Set up an enchantment table, bookshelves, a brewing stand, a cauldron and a chest full of supplies like lapis lazuli, blaze powder and potion ingredients.

UNDERWATER FARM

Most food sources and plants are only found back on dry land, so it's worth taking the time to build yourself an underwater farm. That way, if you run out of wood or have a sudden craving for cookies you'll be able to remedy the situation without returning to the surface.

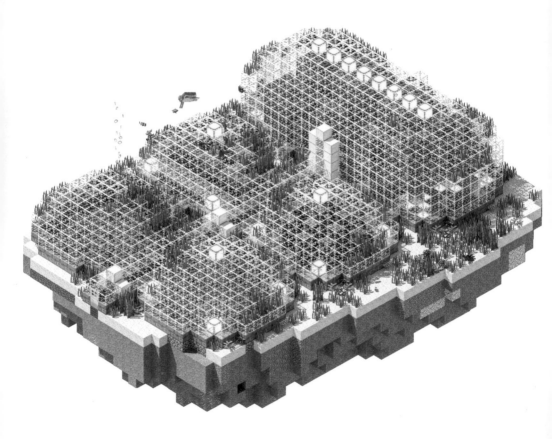

YOU WILL NEED:

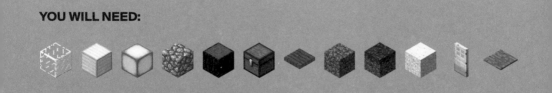

SCHEMATICS

These plans show the underwater farm from various perspectives so you can see how it's built. It's enclosed in a large glass structure that looks a bit like a greenhouse, and divided into several sections for different crops.

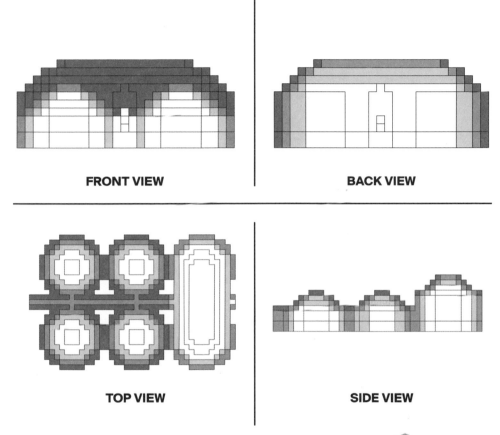

FRONT VIEW

BACK VIEW

TOP VIEW

SIDE VIEW

IDEAL LOCATION

You'll need a fair bit of space to accommodate this farm, so find a clear area of ocean floor near your house or base. You could even join the farm onto the side of your house so you can access it safely whenever you like.

OCEAN

UNDERWATER FARM STRUCTURE

 Enclose your farm in a glass structure so you can keep an eye on it from outside. This design looks like several dome-shaped greenhouses from the outside, but they're joined together by a long walkway down the middle.

 Connecting your crop farm to your underwater base ensures you can always access it safely. You could build a tunnel linking the two structures or build the farm directly to the side of your base so you can visit your farm whenever you like.

Make sure you can access all areas of your farm without having to trample over seeds by constructing pathways between all the sections.

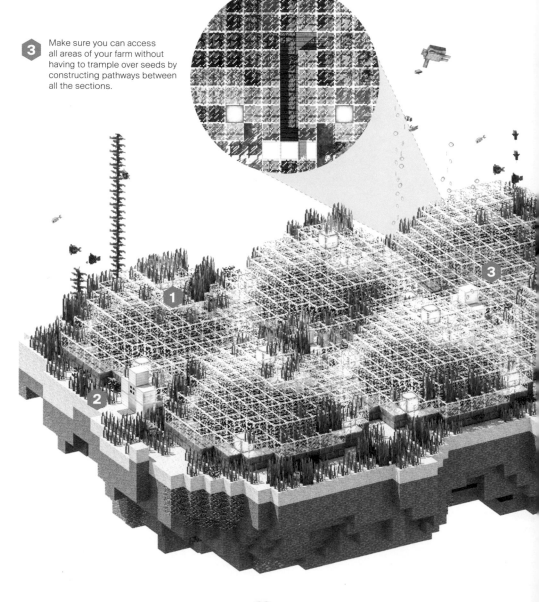

This farm consists of several 9 x 9 areas, each containing a different plant or crop. Turn the page for a reminder of the growing conditions each plant or crop requires in order to thrive.

 Most plants and crops need light to grow, so make sure every area of your farm is lit with sea lanterns or torches. Mushrooms are an exception – there's more info about mushrooms on page 70.

PLANTS AND CROPS

 You can grow wheat, carrots, potatoes and beetroot in the usual way. Place dirt blocks and till them using a hoe, then plant wheat seeds, carrots, potatoes and beetroot seeds. Make sure each plant is at most 4 blocks away from water – the block in the center of each field is a water block covered with a trapdoor.

2 Mushrooms usually prefer the dark, but plant them on podzol or mycelium blocks and they'll grow at any light level. You can find mycelium in mushroom field biomes and podzol in giant tree taiga biomes. Mycelium can only be mined with a tool enchanted with silk touch, otherwise it will just drop dirt.

You'll need melons if you want to craft glistering melon so that you can brew potion of healing. Melon seeds can be planted in tilled dirt and will need to be within 4 blocks of water. You'll also need to leave 1 empty block of dirt next to each plant for the melon to grow into.

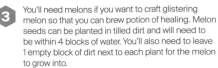 Plant oak saplings in dirt to provide you with a renewable source of wood. Saplings will need at least 4 empty blocks above them. Try spacing them 4 blocks apart so they have plenty of space to grow. Oak saplings are better than other types of sapling because the leaves may drop apples when broken.

 You'll need sugar to make fermented spider eye, which in turn is needed to brew various potions. Plant sugar canes on dirt, podzol or sand right next to water.

 You don't need an entire jungle tree to grow cocoa beans – a few blocks of jungle wood will be enough. Place cocoa beans on the side of jungle wood and a new cocoa pod will form. Remember to wait until the pod is an orange-brown color before you harvest it or it won't drop anything. You can then craft cocoa beans with wheat to make cookies. Yum!

OCEAN OBSERVATORY

Now that you have plenty of experience building underwater, why not go one step further and construct an entire ocean observatory? This expansive structure allows you to study ocean life from complete safety.

YOU WILL NEED:

SCHEMATICS

These plans show the ocean observatory from various perspectives so you can see how it's constructed. The entrance is above sea level but the observatory sits just above the ocean floor.

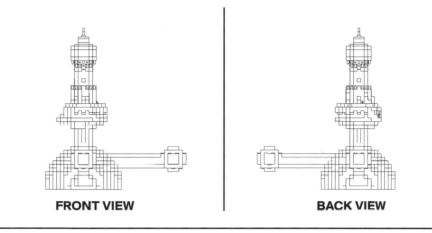

FRONT VIEW   **BACK VIEW**

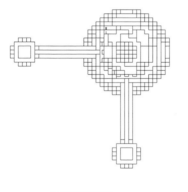

TOP VIEW

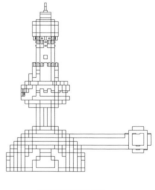

SIDE VIEW

OCEAN

IDEAL LOCATION

This observatory can be built anywhere, but the ideal location would be at the boundary between two or more different areas of ocean. That way, you can study the widest possible variety of ocean life without having to leave the observatory.

OCEAN OBSERVATORY EXTERIOR

1 The entrance to the observatory is above sea level, on an island that can be reached by boat. The entrance also doubles as a lighthouse with a giant glowstone lamp at the top, so it's easy to spot at night.

2 Much of the observatory is made from glass so inhabitants can see what's going on in the ocean around them. Bright orange and blue concrete blocks have been used to construct the framework. This makes it easy to spot.

A large concrete dome lies at the center of the observatory. It has two floors – the bottom floor is open so you can swim out into the ocean.

 Several glass tunnels lead from the central dome to smaller stations. These stations have been built in particularly interesting areas of ocean – above a ravine that produces bubble columns, for example, and next to some underwater ruins.

OCEAN OBSERVATORY INTERIOR

 A crafting area has been set up on the top floor of the central dome. Inhabitants can craft, brew and enchant all the supplies they need to go on ocean expeditions.

2 Near the crafting area is a kitchen where explorers can cook any fish they've collected. There are also stores of other food items here like steak, pork chops and cake.

3 The bottom floor of the central dome has no base and is open to the ocean. It looks a bit like a swimming pool from above, but swim downward and you'll find yourself in open ocean. Ladders are positioned every few blocks around the pool to help divers climb in and out. Be careful – drowned mobs might be able to climb up these ladders, so keep an eye out for unwanted guests.

4 The observatory is lit with sea lanterns. These have been used sparingly so that the observatory isn't too much brighter than the ocean around it.

5 A staircase connects the top floor to the bottom floor of the central dome so inhabitants can travel between the two.

6 Tridents and swords are stored in this area. Anyone intending to go on an ocean expedition can pick up whatever they need from these chests.

FINAL WORDS

Well then, now you're looking ready to jump in! You must be feeling pretty excited about getting to practice everything you've learned. Take care down there, and we wish you the very best of luck in finding every fabulous treasure the ocean can offer. Thanks for playing!

ALEX WILTSHIRE
THE MOJANG TEAM

STAY IN THE KNOW!

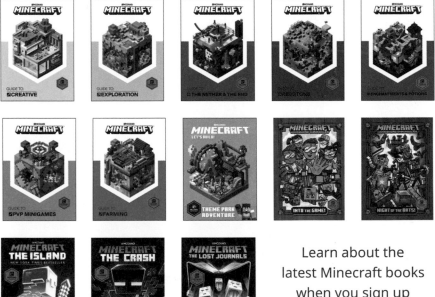